Soar To Success - *Minus the Stress*

(Proven Strategies to Reduce Your Stress)

Published by Sam Hester

Houston, Texas

Contact

sam@geezerfitness.net

geezerfitness.net

Copyright ©2008

Sam Hester,

All Rights Reserved.

ISBN: 978-0-615-23238-6

All rights reserved. No part of this book may be reproduced in any form except for the brief quotation in review, without permission in writing from the author/publisher.

Please check with your physician before undertaking any type of exercise program, or before utilizing any stress relief information or technique in this book if you have any concerns. The information here is of a general nature based upon the author's experience, and should not be substituted for medical advice.

Contents

1. Introduction-pg. 5
2. Stay In the Arena-pg. 7
3. Research-pg. 11
4. What is Stress?-pg. 13
5. Chronic Stress-pg. 18
6. Our Minds-pg. 20
7. Stress Card-pg. 23
8. Do Something Physical-pg. 26
9. Change Your Breathing-pg. 29
10. Progressive Relaxation-pg. 39
11. Visualization/Imagery-pg. 41
12. Meditation-pg. 45
13. Affirmations-pg. 49
14. Conclusion-pg. 51

Introduction

Hello. My name is Sam Hester, and over the last 25 years working as a counselor, coach, speaker, author, researcher, consultant, and trainer I have learned a lot about stress.

During this period, I have worked with thousands of individuals and I've found that what holds many people back in life is not a lack of education, knowledge, or skills, but the effects of stress. Stress that blocks you from tapping into the abilities you already have.

If you were drawn to this book, you're probably a person with a number of responsibilities along with a good deal of talent and ambition. I believe that everything you need to soar to success is already inside you. If you clear away your stress, you'll clear the path to accessing your own gifts.

As a researcher, I have studied volumes of material on stress. Doctors and scientists have produced much data describing why you become stressed and over the centuries, philosophers, religious leaders and spiritual masters have taught how to initiate relaxation, but few have put the information all together in a simple, comprehensive way, such as you'll read in this short book.

I can assure you, the stress reduction techniques I'm going to teach you are very effective. As a part of a research study that I conducted – the participants using these same techniques – reported reducing their stress levels by up to 33% over a three-month period of time.

I have distilled the most successful tools into a few key techniques that I'm passing on to you. I'm going to preface these techniques with some background on your physiology. This will give you a picture of how stress affects you physically, why you have it and what happens to your grateful body when you relieve it of stress.

Stay In the Arena

In 1910, President Teddy Roosevelt, a true Renaissance man and author of 35 books, gave a speech at the Sorbonne entitled *"The Man in The Arena."* In this speech, he said:

> "It is not the critic who counts; not the man who points out where
>
> the doer of deeds could have done them better. The credit belongs
>
> to the man who is actually in the arena, whose face is marred by
>
> dust and sweat and blood ..."

Right now, as you go about your work and tend to your responsibilities, you are in the arena, and I have good news: you don't have to leave the arena of your life to manage your stress. There is no need to attend seminars, travel to an Ashram or seek weekly therapy. You can read this work and immediately begin to utilize the tools I give you. They will also enhance your enjoyment of the place you are in right now in your life, as you work to increase your success.

Stress is a hot topic these days, but much of the information available to you is either too broad, or too complicated, and the subject as covered in the media often does a disservice by focusing on changing your external environment.

Many of the tips don't go far enough, or have been replaced with new techniques by the time you hear them. Besides, most of you have already changed many of the external things that you can.

What has brought about the current emphasis on stress, anyway? Since the 1940s, America has seen an explosion in so-called "lifestyle" related health issues, including obesity, hypertension, heart disease and diabetes, but, why?

The answer is found in both ancient history and modern habits. What it comes down to is that our behavior has gotten way out of sync with what our bodies were designed to handle. We live sedentary lives while our bodies constantly kick into stress responses that were inherent in primitive man.

These responses were in keeping with the strenuous activity and the life threatening conditions he had to deal with. With the physiology of a much more active human being, it's no wonder that you have difficulty relaxing. This, of course, has a cascading effect on the rest of your life.

Because of stress, many of you are living well below your potential, just going through the motions of life. You may have begun to wonder, *is this all there is*? An often-quoted observation by Henry Thoreau in the 19th century was, *"Most men live lives of quiet desperation."* Taking this commentary on mankind's stress and depression forward 150 years to the present, his remark is, sadly, more on target now than ever.

Research

In fact, here are some facts to prove it. American businesses suffer an estimated $400 billion a year in stress-related loss to productivity, or, about $10 thousand per employee. Almost 100 million people in this country take medication for a stress related illness, and the American Medical Association states that at least 80 percent of all illnesses have some stress-related component.

We now know that stress is actually life threatening. You've heard about the mind-body connection, but there was very little scientific evidence to support the concept until 2004.

That year, a report came out on the work of Dr. Elisa Epel, a psychiatrist and researcher from the University of California at San Francisco. Dr. Epel's research revealed the first direct link between psychological stress and the aging process at the molecular level.

Her study involved women between the ages of 20 and 50 who were healthy, but who had kids with horrific illnesses such as autism and cerebral palsy. These mothers were involved in non-stop care giving.

The women were given a series of tests that focused on telomeres, the caps on the end of each human chromosome. Telomeres are like a cellular clock of aging. When your cells divide, your telomeres get shorter, and when your cells cannot divide anymore death occurs.

Interestingly, the women who self reported the most stress over the longest period of time correlated with the ones who did the worst on the tests.

In the study, women who reported the most stress had telomeres equivalent to women 10 years older than themselves. This landmark study gave evidence that, when you are stressed, your body is literally in a state of deterioration.

What is Stress?

Now let's look at stress in your own life: your boss, your job, your kids, your spouse. Each one is a stimulus, and it's your response to the stimulus that actually causes you stress, but, if you think for a minute, I'll bet you'll agree that most of the things that stress you, also bring you joy. It just depends on how you perceive your boss, your job, your family, at that moment.

My definition of stress is this: it's your body's internal, physiological reaction to *perceived* outside threats. Notice the word "perceived." A particular form of stimulation that bothers you, might not bother me, and vice versa.

You can actually pinpoint where stress comes from on a physiological level. If you put your hand on the back of your head, just above your neck, this is where your body's central nervous system is housed.

In the sympathetic branch of your involuntary central nervous system, your stress reaction is produced. Imagine: you can put your hand right on the area in your body where all that turmoil starts!

Your stress reaction is nature's way of saying beware and pay attention. But nature and your body don't tell you *what* to beware of. It is like the alarm going off in your house, but you are not sure if it's because of a fire, a break-in, or false alarm. It just gets your attention and makes you alert.

Let me describe what happens when your stress reaction goes off. Let's say you're driving along and a kid runs out in front of your car. In a fraction of a second, you move your foot off the gas and hit the brake. You didn't have to **think** about this, you just naturally react to a stimulus so that you won't hit the child.

In that fraction of a second, your adrenal glands start kicking out adrenalin, your heart can jump 30 beats, your blood pressure rises, and your breathing turns rapid and shallow. In addition, the blood travels away from your limbs and the outer part of your body into your core, to keep glucose and oxygen going to your brain. Non-essential organ systems, like digestion, actually start shutting down in descending order of survival.

*This is called an **acute** stress reaction.* It keeps your body functioning while you're in distress, but it is hard on your body. Shallow breathing alone deprives you of 30 per cent of your available oxygen. It is no wonder every time you experience this kind of reaction, it contributes to the aging process.

The insidious thing about an acute stress reaction is that it will happen automatically, with or without your willing participation. So when it comes to reducing stress, awareness and information on how your body operates under pressure can be very helpful.

When you have an acute stress reaction, nature assumes that within a very short period of time, you are going to engage your large muscle groups and move like hell. That behavior has been ingrained in humans for hundreds of thousand of years, and today it is called the *fight-or-flight response.*

But when was the last time that you actually ran away from your boss when he or she stressed you out? When was the last time you got into a fight over criticism of a report you wrote at work? You don't react like that! Instead, you sit still, just like the chameleon when threatened – you freeze. So, the actual sequence for humans is *fight, flight or freeze*, just as it is in the animal kingdom. You sit in your office, car and home, having hundreds or thousands of these acute stress responses every day, and you wonder why you feel like crap.

The problem is not the acute stress reaction itself. The harm comes from the build up of numerous acute stress reactions over time. The effect of this build-up is called ***chronic* stress**. It results from the accumulation of powerful stress hormones, specifically adrenaline and cortisol. *Chronic stress is the bottom line stress problem for us humans.*

Chronic Stress

It is astounding to think that seven out of ten of the most popular prescriptions that doctors routinely prescribe are to help counteract various ailments related to chronic stress. You know the conditions I mean. They include depression, anxiety, irritable bowel syndrome and hypertension. Having worked in healthcare for 20 years, I do agree there are legitimate reasons for using drugs for these problems; especially where genetic factors come into play, such as hypertension and high cholesterol, however, as I said at the outset, the root of today's stress epidemic is our inactive lifestyle. It simply no longer calls for the intense stress reactions that our bodies produce.

For instance, have you ever come into the office and found 200 unanswered emails? You probably feel overwhelmed and don't know where to begin. More than likely you have too much cortisol on a part of your brain called the hippocampus, which is involved with decision making and learning.

The reaction you're having would have been appropriate if you were hunting for food and had to enter a pitch black forest filled with loud animal noises with only one spear on you.

Our Mind

Outside stimulus aside, your mind alone can be the bearer of stress. To give you an idea, I'd like you to close your eyes for a minute, and picture the worst boss you've ever had. Focus on what it felt like, working for that person: anxiety, knots in your stomach, resentment gnawing at you. Stay with that person's image for a minute and feel the feelings. Then, picture the best boss you've ever had. Remember how it felt, working for this great boss: more relaxed and peaceful, even secure. Did you notice a distinct difference in your body, thinking of these two people?

It is estimated that the average American has 60,000 random thoughts a day and any one of them can cause your body to respond, positively or negatively. Think of how many acute stress reactions your mind is creating every 24 hours; thousands, perhaps, and you're not even aware of them. As I said, your body doesn't ask for permission to react. It just reacts.

Earlier, I mentioned that the acute stress response is produced in the sympathetic branch of your involuntary nervous system. The other branch of your involuntary nervous system is the *parasympathetic*, where the "relaxation response" is produced. You may have heard of the relaxation response as heralded in Dr. Herbert Benson's book of the 1970's.

The relaxation response, as your body's counterpoint to the stress reaction, is an excellent example of how the body is always seeking homeostasis, or balance.

Many people believe that the relaxation response is outside their ability to control. But that isn't the case. Look at it this way: when you feel warm in your house, which is a stimulus, and you consciously get out of your chair and turn down the thermostat, that is a response. The **result** is that you feel cooler and more comfortable. Isn't it good to know that, in the same way, you can turn on your relaxation response at almost any time and any place, with the result of feeling less stressed?

The relaxation techniques I'll teach you will do just that – set your relaxation response in motion. As far as we know, the human being is the only species in the world that can consciously overcome their physiology in such a way.

Stress Card

Have you ever noticed, when you're very stressed, your hands get cold? When you have an acute stress reaction, the blood tends to go away from your limbs into the main body cavity. This keeps oxygen and blood going to your brain, and the lack of blood in your limbs lowers the temperature of those areas. Conversely, where there is a pooling of blood, there is warmth. In fact, your hand temperature can vary up to about 40 degrees, from 60 to 100 degrees Fahrenheit.

To check this out, take the stress card and look at the front. You will see a square and a set of four different colors. If you're a geezer like I am, you remember the mood rings that were popular in the 1960's and 1970's that we used to check out what mood our friends were in.

Although the stress card looks like a toy, it does have an actual clinical usage in measuring the temperature of your hand, if you use it indoors.

Now, put your thumb on the square for about 20 seconds and then remove it. If the card color is black, it means that your skin temperature is less than 80 degrees, which indicates that you are feeling pretty tense. If the card is red, your skin temperature is about 84, meaning you are somewhat nervous. The color green says that your skin is 87 degrees and you are feeling calm. A deep blue color indicates a skin temperature of over 91, in which case you are outright relaxed!

Whatever the color is, it is just a snapshot of your hand temperature at this moment, kind of like an overnight poll in a political race. If you'll excuse the pun, the rule of thumb for this test is: warmer hands, warmer mood. But there can be a number of reasons as to why you show a black or red color, so don't let it bother you.

Now that you know why you become stressed, and how your body reacts internally, let's explore some solutions to stress, and learn how you can change your stress card from black to blue.

Stress Relief

Do Something Physical

The crux of stress management, the big challenge is: how do you intentionally kick on the relaxation process? Even better, how do you engage the relaxation response when there is no direct, outside stressor? If you can learn to do this, to frequently get into a state of relaxation, *it is absolutely the best thing you can do to control your stress.*

The first tool for reducing stress is simply to move. In fact, when you're aware of having a stress reaction, your body is signaling you to do something physical. So, when it is *appropriate* and you are *able*, get up and get active.

You know that when you take a break from your desk for a short walk, you not only feel better, you become more alert and productive. When you move your body, you burn off the stress hormones, such as adrenaline and cortisol, and their effects, just *like the sun burns off the dew in the morning.* It's a case of cause and effect – the simple principle that controls the entire physical world!

In modern times, researchers have found pockets in rural areas of lesser-developed countries where there is little, if any, stress-related disease. People in these locales are healthy and very active, right up until they die of old age at 100 or so. Their lifestyle is marked by a high level of physical exercise and almost a total absence of stress as we define it today.

As I mentioned, the idea of returning to leading *primitive* lives is not very realistic. But, keeping in mind that our bodies were initially meant to move many miles a day, a case can definitely be made for increasing our daily activity.

The research on the subject of exercise is very interesting. In 1996, the U.S. Surgeon General's report on physical activity and health noted that people who participated in several brief exercise periods per day – for example, walking 3 times a day for 10 minutes – had the same cardio-respiratory improvement as individuals who walked for 30 minutes straight. The message was that to benefit from exercise, you don't have to devote big chunks of time to it.

The Surgeon General's report also said that women who were in a walking program during several periods per day, stuck to their programs more than those women who exercised only once a day.

There is also anecdotal evidence that by walking just a total of 10 minutes a day, you can lower your blood pressure, body mass index and improve your overall health. From a stress perspective, *any* movement is good.

One other important note about exercise" the *sooner* that you can get up and move after you feel stress, the better. It is like cleaning up a spill as soon as it hits the carpet.

Change Your Breathing

Now, let's try something even easier to reduce your stress, which is breathing.

There is a popular product selling in the media and on the internet that includes a self-administered blood pressure machine and a CD that teaches you to breathe correctly. The object is to lower your blood pressure.

This seems to be a reputable product that physicians have endorsed, but the results you get with the breathing techniques that I am going to give you are the same, and they cost much less than the $300 you would have to pay for the other product.

I mentioned before that when you have a stress reaction and your body automatically goes into overdrive, one thing that happens is a change in your breathing. It becomes rapid, shallow, noisy and irregular. The insidious thing about stress is that you don't have to be consciously aware for it to occur. In this case, your breathing just increases automatically.

The stress reaction maintains a sufficient supply of glucose and oxygen to the brain to make quick decisions for survival. Of course, this was never meant to be a permanent state, but for humans today, it often is.

Think about what happens when you're in your car going up a steep hill and you press your foot down hard on the accelerator. You want instant power to get up the hill, and when you reach the top, you back off the accelerator. Likewise, many of you are keeping the foot on the accelerator of your life. You stay in a constant state of overdrive – through worry, pushing yourself too hard, eating improperly and not exercising, to name a few activities. Then you wonder why your engine – your body – isn't in good shape.

Nature assumed that life was not going to be all hills all the time; that after the immediate need for extra energy had passed, your body would return to normal, and in primitive man, that was what happened. After the genuine threat had passed, a person returned to a naturally relaxed state. Those were the good old days!

Now, let's try a breathing technique that is an easy way to jump-start your relaxation response.

I'd like you to close your eyes and put your hand on your stomach. Now, breathe in slowly, taking a deep breath, and push your stomach out all the way. Then, use your abdominal muscles to pull your stomach in all the way back as far as you can, and let all of the air out of your lungs. You may notice that, even though it feels like you have more lung power when you inhale, actually there is more strength in your lungs during the exhalation.

That's it! That's all you need for this technique. Slowly breathe in, pushing your stomach out, and then exhale, squeezing the air out of your lungs. Continue to do this for two minutes.

One dramatic effect of this exercise is how it slows down a racing mind. This is the way your body is meant to breathe all the time, except when you need to act in a crisis

Think of the last time you were on vacation and forgot what day of the week it was! That trip to your favorite place, where everything seemed perfect. When you are in an idyllic situation like that, and your unconscious feels safe and loved, then your breathing *automatically* becomes deep, quiet, slow and regular.

You breathe from your diaphragm and shazam – you feel relaxed.

Remember, you can engage your relaxation response by breathing this way any time, whether you're in a crisis, a normal state, or if your mind starts to think about something disturbing. The most important thing to know – and after you are successful at this, you will know it for sure – is that you can manage your stress this easily.

Alternate Nostril Breathing

Now I want to tell you about another relaxation tool using your breath. It's called alternate nostril breathing and it is one of the most powerful relaxation techniques I know of.

Alternate nostril breathing dates back thousands of years to India, when the yogis believed that our natural breathing had a cycle to it.

They said that during a 2 to 6 hour period, each one of our nostrils would alternate in dominating our breathing, and they changed back and forth in a natural rhythm.

There is research showing that people using this technique score better on the left hemisphere in math and spatial testing and on the right hemisphere in creative processes. From a practical level, alternate nostril breathing enables you to feel both centered and alert.

Let's try it together. Take the index finger on your right hand and gently put it on your right nostril, closing off the nasal passage. Take a deep breath in - through your left nostril.

Now, move the index finger and place it on your left nostril, breathing out slowly through only your right nostril. Leave your finger there. Now breathe in through your right nostril. Move your finger to your right nostril, and then breathe out through your left nostril. This is one compete round.

Do this for several minutes and then stop and see how you feel. If you get light headed, just stop for a few minutes and the sensation will subside shortly.

More than likely, your breathing has been shallow all day, and you were depriving yourself of that 30 per cent of available oxygen that I mentioned earlier. So, a big blast of oxygen to your brain through alternate nostril breathing could make you a little dizzy.

This is a great technique to use when you need to feel balanced and still be alert and productive at work. I suggest you try this several times throughout the day and see how you feel. If you feel better, the return on investment is pretty incredible.

I enjoy teaching this to large groups of people, because I can see a whole room full of faces and bodies relaxing at once.

4-7-8 Technique

Next, I want to teach you what is called the 4-7-8 technique. It is used very successfully to treat panic attacks and anxiety disorders. I have taught it to thousands of people and, invariably, it is the most potent tool in my stress management kit. It supercharges your relaxation response and it is guaranteed to help you feel less stressed within just a few minutes.

Dr. Andrew Weil, a Harvard educated physician, and one of the top wellness doctors in the country, actually prescribes this for his patients. He believes that by using the 4-7-8 technique over time, it is possible to actually reset your autonomic nervous system and counteract a number of bodily complaints that are related to stress.

Now, with this breathing exercise, you are going to *breathe in through your nose to the count of four, hold your breath to the count of seven, and then somewhat forcefully exhale from your mouth to the count of eight.* This is one complete round. Be sure to keep your count even throughout the round.

Try this for 10 rounds and see how you feel. Again, you might get dizzy from the super oxygenation you're experiencing. If so, just stop, and come back to this exercise several times a day. If you are having trouble going to sleep, this is a powerful elixir that can put you out pretty fast. So, DO NOT use this technique if you have to drive or operate heavy machinery in the next hour.

Progressive Relaxation

Now that you have activated your relaxation response with your breathing, let's look at some other tools to help you relax.

When you feel stress, the muscles utilize the stress hormones that I have already mentioned. They provide the energy to get you the hell out of Dodge, but the continual pumping out of these hormones, or corticosteroids, into your nervous system, causes your muscles to retain these and many other neurotoxins that are meant to help you deal with immediate danger. If you are worried about the steroids in our beef supply, imagine what is accumulating in your own muscles.

That brings us to massage, which is a great tool for managing stress. A good massage releases those toxins from your muscles; then they are picked up by the lymphatic system and eliminated from your body. If you can't get a professional massage often, here is something else that can help you get rid of built-up, stress-related toxins.

Lie on your back – preferably on the floor, but the couch, recliner or bed will do. If you need support for your back, put a pillow under your legs. Close your eyes. Now, ball your fists and squeeze all of your muscles from your head to your toes at the same time, and hold it.

Make a scowling face, squeeze your butt muscles, and really tighten everything for about 5 seconds, then relax and let it all go. Be sure to take slow, deep breaths, to help release the toxins.

This is called progressive relaxation. So, on the next cycle, you're going to tighten your muscles and hold them for about 10 seconds, and then relax. Continue this exercise for two minutes. At that point, you should feel noticeably more relaxed.

Any time you feel tense, you can close your office door and do this routine for a couple of minutes. You'll find it helps you be more productive during the day.

Visualization / Imagery

So, we've gone through several ways to initiate your relaxation response through physical means.

Now I want to tell you about addressing stress on a mental level. I'm going to start with a technique called visualization.

Much of what I read about this subject is complicated and confusing, so it is my intention to make it easy.

You remember earlier, I had you think about a good boss and then a bad boss, and focus on how you felt. When you create a "mental picture" like that, you get to be your own photographer and *choose* what you take a snap shot of.

Let's try an exercise. Sit back in a comfortable position and relax. Breathe slowly and deeply. Now, think of being in a very special place, perhaps with a special person, where you are totally relaxed and in the present moment.

Next, close your eyes and focus on this experience. Focus *on how it feels in your body*. That is the secret. If you are at the beach, feel the warm sun, hear the waves, smell the fresh sea air, and *be in the experience* – not just observing it.

So, this is a three-step process: Choose the picture, hold it in your mind, and focus on how it feels, as if you were really there.

There is evidence to suggest that, during this exercise, your body doesn't actually know whether you are at that special place or not. That is pretty amazing. So is the fact that if you keep photos of your loved ones around, you actually get a positive relaxation response when you look at them. The guiding principle in visualization is, the more positive pictures you put in your mind, the more positive responses you will experience in your body.

Now, I want to say a word about what is called *"guided imagery."* Perhaps you have been to a workshop, or bought a CD, where you get relaxed and listen to some soothing music, and focus on the voice of the presenter.

He starts with a generic positive image, like a beach scene. Then, following his lead, you create a *series* of "mind pictures" that flow like a movie strip, one after another, such as walking down the beach, seeing a beautiful sunset and other positive pictures.

This is a very helpful technique and you can do it on your own, without someone talking you through it. Start with a positive picture that is good for you, and let your imagination wander. It is really that simple – just dream away!

Meditation

Meditation is another relaxation tool involving your mind, but the goal here is to quiet your mind, instead of creating images with it.

I'd say that meditation is one of the most misunderstood stress management practices there is. This is partly because it has been shrouded in so called "Eastern philosophy." Also, it is my observation that, as presented by metaphysicians, meditation doesn't tend to yield immediate benefits, which adds to its lack of appeal.

So, what exactly is meditation? It is the act of getting quiet, turning off all outside stimulation and going inside yourself. According to religious and spiritual teachings, that is where you will find the "answers" to all of your questions and problems. There is no right or wrong way to meditate. You don't have to sit on the floor in an uncomfortable or weird position.

A comfortable chair or recliner is fine. Finding a meditation practice that works for you is partly trial and error, but I will share with you a simple focusing technique that is helpful to many. This technique involves a mantra, or focusing word.

The purpose of a mantra is to provide your conscious mind with a distraction, to minimize the random thoughts that come and go all the time. The mantra makes it easier to clear your mind and go into an Alpha brain state. In meditation, that is the state you want to be in.

The teachings of yoga tell us that the mind and breath are twin brothers.

What happens to one happens to the other. Meditation is a good example of this. By relaxing your body and mind with breathing, you are much more likely to be successful at meditating.

I remember trying to meditate 25 years ago, without incorporating slow, deep breathing. It was very hard for me to relax enough to meditate successfully.

Natural Mantra – So' Ham

Let's try this method of meditation. It's called So' Ham, which is the mantra you use. Sitting with your feet flat on the floor, get comfortable and use the 4-7-8 breathing technique for 3 - 5 minutes to get relaxed. Then, breathing slowly, on the outgoing breath, say to yourself the word "**So**" or "Sooooo…" drawing out the word for the entire exhalation.

On the <u>incoming</u> breath, silently say to yourself "**Ham**" or "Haammm...." drawing out the word for the entire inhalation.

So' Ham has been described as the natural mantra, as it is the closest sound to our relaxed breathing pattern. It is translated from antiquity to mean, "I am that."

If this doesn't feel comfortable, and you want to try something else, here is another suggestion.

Breathing slowly on the <u>outgoing</u> breath, say to yourself the word "**Now**"..."Nooow," drawing out the word for the entire exhalation.

On the <u>incoming</u> breath, say to yourself "**Yes**" or "Yesss...." drawing out the word for the entire inhalation. You can use any words that you like, but these do nicely, because "Yes" is the most positive word in the language and "Now" affirms that you are in the present.

You can do this meditation for as little or as long as you like. A general guideline is to start with five minutes a day and work up to 20.

Practicing meditation can make you feel more centered, so when the slings and arrows come at you during the day, you have fewer and less severe stress reactions. Meditation is an excellent preventive tool against stress.

Affirmations

The last stress management practice I'll share with you is the use of affirmations. An affirmation is a short, positive statement beginning with the word "I," or, "My."

You may have noticed how your mind naturally tends to gravitate towards what is wrong in your life, but, by affirming positive ideas out loud, you can provide your subconscious mind with positive self-images to help counteract the bad ones.

Much has been written about affirmations, and you can find them in many books. But the best ones are the ones you create for yourself.

Here is the secret: you need to make them *personal, positive and in the present*. Remember to begin with the words "I" or "My" and to use positive wording.

For example, you would say, "I am feeling relaxed," instead of, "I am not stressed."

Here are some other affirmations for reducing stress:

- My body and my mind are one.
- I have enough time to do everything I need today.
- I love myself.
- My life is very rewarding.
- I choose to be happy.

It is good to say your affirmations out loud several times a day, and also to turn to them when you are presented with a stressful stimulus, including your own negative thoughts.

Conclusion

These techniques I have shared with you will give you tremendous benefits in triggering your relaxation response, whether in direct reaction to stress, or in taking action to prevent it from occurring.

In addition, the information I've covered on how your body works will help you bring your body, mind and soul into cooperation with your efforts at stress reduction.

In my work with people of all ages, I have seen that minimizing the impact of stress in your daily life goes a long way toward helping you reach your goals and achieve your dreams. I wish you every good fortune in your journey to success, minus the stress.

www.ingramcontent.com/pod-product-compliance
Lightning Source LLC
Chambersburg PA
CBHW061515040426
42450CB00008B/1634